Seasons of the Moon
AUTUMN MOON

ALSO BY JEAN CRAIGHEAD GEORGE

Seasons of the Moon

AUTUMN MOON

JEAN CRAIGHEAD GEORGE

HARPERTROPHY®

AN IMPRINT OF HARPERCOLLINSPUBLISHERS

Autumn Moon
Copyright © 2001 by Julie Productions, Inc.
Originally published as individual volumes:
The Moon of the Deer text copyright © 1969, 1992
by Jean Craighead George
The Moon of the Alligators text copyright © 1969, 1991
by Jean Craighead George
The Moon of the Gray Wolves text copyright © 1969, 1991
by Jean Craighead George

Library of Congress Cataloging-in-Publication Data
George, Jean Craighead, 1919–
    Autumn moon / Jean Craighead George.
        p.   cm. (Seasons of the moon ; v. 1)
    Works originally published from 1967 to 1969 in series: The Thirteen
moons.
    Includes biographical references (p.).
    Contents: The moon of the deer — The moon of the alligators —
The moon of the gray wolves.
    ISBN 0-06-442172-4 (pbk.)
    1. Deer—Juvenile literature. 2. White-tailed deer—Connecticut—
Juvenile literature. 3. Alligators—Juvenile literature. 4. Alligators—
Florida—Everglades—Juvenile literature. 5. Wolves—Juvenile literature.
6. Wolves—Alaska—Juvenile literature. [1. Autumn. 2. Deer.
3. Alligators. 4. Wolves.] I. Title.
QL795.D3 G395 2001
599.65'2—dc21
                                                            00-054232
                                                                  CIP
                                                                  AC

Book design by Andrea Simkowski
❖
First Harper Trophy edition, 2001
Visit us on the World Wide Web!
www.harperchildrens.com

CONTENTS

WHY IS THIS SERIES CALLED
SEASONS OF THE MOON?

Each year there are either thirteen full or thirteen new moons. This series is named in honor of the four seasons of the thirteen moons of the year.

Our culture, which bases its calendar year on sun-time, has no names for the thirteen moons. I have named the thirteen lunar months after thirteen North American animals. Primarily night prowlers, these animals, at a particular time of the year in a particular place, do wondrous things. The places are known to you, but the animal moon names are not because I made them up. So that you can

place them on our sun calendar, I have identi-
fied them with the names of our months.
When I ran out of these, I gave the thirteenth
moon, the Moon of the Moles, the expand-
able name December–January.

Fortunately, the animals do not need
calendars, for names or no names, sun-time, or
moon-time, they follow their own inner clocks.

—JEAN CRAIGHEAD GEORGE

Seasons of the Moon
AUTUMN MOON

THE MOON OF THE DEER

The full moon of September rose at a few minutes past six in the evening. The huge orange globe, which seemed to be lit from within, was called the Harvest Moon, the moon of the autumnal equinox. It came up as the sun went down, a phenomenon that gives farmers extra light by which to harvest their crops before the killing frost comes.

For the young males of the white-tailed deer, the all-night moon was the moon of challenge.

Across southern Canada, the United States, and Mexico (with the exception of

California, Nevada, and Utah), the one-and-a-half-year-old bucks were each sporting two daggerlike antlers. They snorted as they sharpened them on trees and bushes. Challenges were ahead.

One of these young bucks was a resident of Mamacoke Marsh, on the Connecticut shore. Golden-gray in color with large, heavily lashed eyes, he stood in the moonlight on a wooded hill above his span of the tidal marshes. Beyond the marshes stretched the bay and, farther out to sea, the barrier islands.

The young buck was looking down on the continent's end. Here the sea mingled with rippling grasses to make one of the earth's most valuable natural resources. Like all salt marshes, it was a nursery for ocean fish and a food source for the vast variety of life that lives in the estuaries and bays.

At midnight the young buck was resting in the groundsel-tree patch and chewing his cud.

Like all deer, he was usually abroad only in the dawn and twilight, but the constant light from the Harvest Moon permitted him to wander from moonrise to moonset. The sound of heavy hoofbeats alerted him. An enormous buck was coming his way. The young buck's long, sensitive nose, which could pick up at least a million odors we will never know, tingled with the zestful scent of the eight-pointer, the largest and most aggressive white-tailed deer in the Mamacoke Marsh.

The marsh seemed an unlikely home for deer, with its tides and salt water; but it was, in fact, an Eden for the deer. Just behind the beach grew a seaside garden of wildflowers— sea lavender, purple gerardia, seaside golden- rod and saltwort—that the deer grazed in summer and early September. On higher and drier soil grew the salt-meadow grass and cordgrass, rich in minerals and vitamins. Even higher grew the switch grass, whose seeds the deer ate. At the land side of the tidal marsh, elder bushes and groundsel trees gave shelter and browse to the deer. Westward of this community of plants stood the oak woods, and beyond them the pines. The marsh was home not only to the deer, but to sparrows, shorebirds, geese, muskrats, raccoons, and otters. It fed millions of shorebirds, geese, and ducks as they migrated back and forth from their breeding to their wintering grounds.

The tempo of the hoofbeats in the groundsel trees increased. The eight-point buck was trotting the young buck's way. The young buck felt the challenge of his new antlers and walked forward to meet him. The older buck grunted a warning. The young one hesitated. Then he moved into the cordgrass and stopped.

The world at his feet was teeming with insects, crabs, snails, spiders, birds, and worms, for the cordgrass nourishes most of the life in the marsh. When the tide comes in, tons of plant minerals dissolve in the water. As it goes out, the minerals and organic material fertilize the channels and estuaries as well as the bays and ocean. Tidal marshes produce ten times as much food as any comparable area on land—fish, scallops, blue crabs, quahogs, and soft-shell clams, by the millions of tons. The white-tailed deer herd of Mamacoke Marsh had inherited a wealthy land.

The groundsel trees cracked, and the magnificent head and antlers of the old buck were thrust into view. They gleamed in the moonlight. In seeming madness, the young buck lowered his head in challenge. His little spikes shone like silver daggers. They had begun to bud in April and had grown all summer under a soft skin called velvet. By early September the spikes were hard and fully developed. Only a few days ago the spike buck had scratched the last tag of velvet from one spike and had polished them both on the trunk of a tree. Now he had turned from a gentle browser into a fighting warrior. He had charged the trees and chased the sea gulls. He had pawed the ground. He had run thirty-five miles an hour, jumped thirty feet horizontally, and leaped eight and a half feet in the air. He had rushed up to meet other spike bucks, lowered his head, and clanked weapons with them half-heartedly. They were still adolescents and not eager to fight.

The rutting, or mating, season was a month away. From late October through February, the older bucks would battle with their antlers to win and then protect their harems, female deer. They began this ritual in September by chasing off the spike bucks. The young bucks were easy to conquer. The spike buck of Mamacoke Marsh was a case in point. The old buck stepped out of the groundsel trees. The spike buck lowered his head to challenge him. The monarch snorted and tossed his huge rack. The sound and sight of the eight-point buck ended the battle. The young buck ran, the white fur under his lifted tail flashing the signal "run, danger." The eight-point buck jogged back into the groundsel trees; but not far.

The spike buck recovered from his scare in the tall cordgrass, which almost reached his shoulders. When he had calmed down, he lowered his head and cropped the seeds. Although he didn't know it, he was meeting another September challenge. His body was demanding a diet that would prepare him for winter—seeds, nuts, fruits, and the twigs of vitamin-rich bushes and trees. Earlier this evening he had smelled hawthorns and sumac inland, but now he dared not pass the eight-point buck to find them. He settled for the seeds of the marsh grasses and the protection of their tall stems.

Several days later the sun rose behind swirling clouds. The spike buck stopped browsing and went to his day bed in the cordgrass. He had not been back to the groundsel trees since the buck had warned him away.

A clapper rail slipped past him and ran into the groundsel tree patch. This was unusual, for the long-necked, slender bird lived far out in the marshes. The spike buck had never seen her anywhere but in the sweet salt-meadow grass and among the reeds and rushes along the tidal channels.

The spike buck could smell her fear. He lifted his head to find her reason for flight. A flock of red-winged blackbirds swept over, around him, and into the groundsel trees. They alighted on the twisted limbs without a sound. Their silence was unusual. Since the crescent moon of September, these birds had been gathering in the marsh by the noisy thousands. They were flocking together in preparation for their fall migration to the southern states. Their silent flight this morning alerted the young buck. The birds often saw enemies before he did. He listened for the sounds of humans.

There were none. The wide, flat marsh was deathly quiet. Even the gulls were not crying as they awakened. The cicadas in the oak forest that usually sang with earsplitting volume in September were silent. The crickets did not rasp their wings together as usual, and the miles of yellowing grass and reeds did not swish.

The spike buck began to feel physically uncomfortable. The atmospheric pressure was dropping. The weight of the air was much less than the normal fifteen pounds per square inch. It was down to twelve pounds per square inch, and affecting his ears and body.

He started back to the groundsel trees, remembered the eight-point buck, and retreated to the edge of a channel that ran out to sea. The tide was low, very low.

A soft rain began to fall. Nearby, a flock of Canada geese gabbled nervously and clustered together. They usually ignored rain, but this morning the atmospheric pressure was making them wary. The birds had left Maine yesterday morning, flying in a V and *honk-a-lonk*ing to keep together. They had arrived at Mamacoke Marsh at dusk. Twenty-five strong, the flock had settled in to rest and eat for a few days before going on down the coast. They would follow the tidal marshes that stretch from Connecticut to Georgia, and overwinter on the ponds, lakes, and marshes in the Southeastern and Gulf states.

More knowledgeable about atmospheric pressure than the inexperienced deer, they began moving inland.

Their nervous gabbling made the spike buck uneasy. He sniffed, twitched his ears, and looked around to better understand their message. No telltale scents came from the land, and no breeze blew off the ocean. He lifted his head. There was no wind at all. Then his senses told him what the birds already knew; a storm was coming. But this was not one of summer's thunderstorms, it was one of September's wild and devastating hurricanes. Born over the tropical ocean, it had gathered strength as it came up the coast over water. Now it was headed for landfall on Connecticut's shore. The pressure dropped lower.

The spike buck turned away from the sea and ran for his groundsel patch, despite the big buck.

As he approached, twigs snapped, and the eight-point buck stepped out into view. In the darkness, his rack loomed black, his nostrils flared. He lowered his antlers—a challenge to fight. The spike buck accepted, lowered his head, and flaunted his spikes. The older buck charged.

When the big hoofs thundered against the ground, the spike buck knew what to do. He turned and sped toward the ocean. White flag up, he bolted across the meadow in twenty-foot bounds, thrashing the seed-filled grass heads wherever his feet went down. The seaside goldenrod nodded in the wind he made.

He ran until he could go no farther. He was on the dunes at the end of the marsh. Beyond boomed heavy storm waves. Shivering, he turned around and walked back to the green reeds where the seaside sparrows made their nests in the spring.

The buck had filled him with fear, but the sight of the marsh was even more terrifying. The channel was almost empty of water, and its muddy bottom gleamed like metal in the stillness. A new kind of enemy was challenging him. He lay down in the reeds to hide from the danger as his mother had taught him to do when he was a fawn.

The drizzle turned to rain. The stillness became more and more ominous. Finally fatigue overcame him, and he tucked his head on his haunch and slept. Around noon he was awakened by a crackling sound in the channel below the reeds. The thousands of fiddler crabs that lived in holes in the bank were noisily blowing and breaking bubbles. The tide had been out so long, they were circulating the water in their mouths to absorb its oxygen and stay alive.

The sea water was far, far out. The low pressure of the hurricane had sucked the water out of the marsh channels and up into the center of the storm, just as liquid is drawn up in a straw when it's sucked on. The column of water in the low-pressure area was a tidal wave—and it was moving landward. As it neared Mamacoke Marsh, the wind started blowing. The rain deluged the coast. The crabs bubbled and snapped. Droves of wildlife abandoned the marsh, and the spike buck once more started back to the groundsel trees. As he neared the sheltered spot, his fear of the monarch stopped him again.

A lone sandpiper ran across the empty channel flats. The bird was not behaving right. It searched and stopped too much, turned around and flicked its wings too frequently. A young bird, it had been running the shores with its parents since June. With the coming of September, the family had flocked with other sandpiper families. Every day they hunted the beaches for sand crabs and sand fleas, then flew out over the ocean and came back. They were warming up for their migration to the Gulf Coast in October.

This morning the lone bird had set out to sea to exercise his wings again. The other sandpipers had not followed. Sensing the coming storm, they had flown up the channel, over the groundsel trees and oaks, and far beyond the pines. When the lone bird returned, he alighted on a deserted beach. He ran, stopped, flicked his wings, and called. Suddenly he screamed his alarm call and flew into the wind.

The cry warned the spike buck. Sensing that he too must act, but afraid to go home, he ran to the edge of the channel. He would swim across to the woods on the other shore; however, there was no water, so he could not swim. He hesitated, for he knew from experience the hazards of the mire on the bottom of the channel. He had sunk up to his ankles in it once. As he stood in the rain, bubbles popped on the surface of the mud as razor-edged and quahog clams burrowed down deep. Their disappearance was not unusual, for each fall they migrated downward to avoid the cold. It was their haste that was alarming.

Too many bubbled too frantically. They were traveling rapidly into the mud to get below the scouring action of the storm waves.

The mussels in the channels had sewn themselves to rocks and to one another with threads of tough mucus, spun from their hidden mouths. This was quite normal. But it was not normal that they were now swiftly spinning even more threads to bind themselves more securely to their moorings.

The spike buck was afraid of the mire and once more started back to the groundsel trees. Again, fear of the eight-point buck over-whelmed him. He walked out to the dunes and into the saltwater grass, one of the plants to grow nearest to the sea. Life is harsh on the beach: The wind blows constantly, soils are poor, and the water is salty. Yet saltwater grass manages to survive these rigors. Its thick leaves hold fresh water as the desert's cacti do. Its roots are shallow and numerous to absorb what little nutrition there is in the sand.

The deer cropped a few watery leaves and lay down. Head up, ears twitching, he let his nose sort out the myriad odors on the wind.

A gull screamed its alarm cry. The grasses whipped and flattened. On land, telephone poles snapped and trees fell. Roofs flew off houses. Then, out beyond the dunes, an ominous roar began. The tidal wave was coming in. On it rode living miles of little fish that had been drawn from the channel and were now riding back to the marsh. The full force of the hurricane was about to strike Mamacoke Marsh.

The spike buck ran inland before the roar. The wind shoved him along. Overhead the lonely sandpiper cried once, then cried no more.

The spike buck came back to the channel edge. He could not go home, and he could not stay. He had no choice but to try to cross the mud flats to the woods south of his groundsel-tree home.

The deer's small cloven hoofs were not designed to walk on mud like the broad hoofs of his bog relative, the moose. Before he had gone many steps, he began to sink. Struggling to free himself, he only sank deeper.

A black duck came running across the mud flat. He was hurrying inland by the easiest route, the waterless channel. Not seeing the buck in the torrential rain, he crashed into him, flapped his wings, and ran up the bank into the reeds.

The spike buck fought to extricate his feet from the mud until he was exhausted. Laying his chin upon the black channel mire, he rested. As he did, calmness and strength returned to him.

Carefully he pulled one front leg out of the mire and stretched it out. Then he eased the other out and, spreading them both as a swimmer would, made himself more buoyant. He did not sink again, but he could not make progress with his legs splayed out.

The wind was now gusting at eighty miles an hour. It was strong enough to blow him away and break his legs if he stood up. Being flat turned out to be a lifesaver. He was so low, he was safe. While the winds raged above him, he pulled his hind legs out of the mud.

With a growl the tidal wave struck the marsh, lifted the young buck up, and carried him landward. In mere seconds he was tossed into the groundsel trees. With him rode driftwood, seaweed, shells and reeds, fish and dead birds.

The spike buck got to his feet and climbed up the groundsel knoll heading for the oak ridge, the highest ground for miles. Even his fear of the eight-point buck no longer held him back. The water was swirling in behind him.

Mice and muskrats deserted their homes in the marsh and scurried up the hill with him. Snakes climbed trees, and raccoons swam toward the forest. Songbirds flew to limbs on the lee side of tree trunks. They shook themselves to keep the driving rain from soaking their feathers.

The young buck reached the top of the groundsel knoll. As tired as he was, he was prepared to fight the eight-point buck. He listened and smelled. Not a deer was anywhere. Trees snapped and bent in the wind, but his herd was gone. They had run inland and were waiting out the storm in a valley in the pine forest.

As the wind and rain raged on, the young buck turned and faced into the hurricane. Sticks flew through the air; the dry elderberries of September hit his nose like darts. He shifted his weight from one hind leg to the other. Late in the afternoon he lay down, but not with any great sense of security. The ocean was still rising. It covered the switch grass and climbed into the groundsel patch—and kept coming.

When the waves lapped his feet, he ran for higher ground in the oak forest. But he did not go far. On the other side of the ground-sel knoll the strange new sea boiled. The knoll was surrounded and would soon be under water. Easing into the flood, he began to swim. Once he touched ground, only to be lifted by a swell and washed back to the groundsel trees. He started off again.

Swimming, fighting to survive, the spike buck rode the next swell into the oaks. He dug in his hoofs and frantically climbed to the top of the ridge. There he collapsed and rested. Suddenly the rain stopped, the winds ceased. The sun came out. Mamacoke Marsh was calm and beautiful. The eye of the hurri-cane had arrived.

He closed his eyelids and slept while the eye of the storm passed, and the rain and wind began again. The southern side of the hurricane was not as violent, and the spike buck slept through it.

Before sunset the next evening, the young buck returned to the marsh. The wind-beaten grasses and reeds had sprung back, and gulls flew overhead hunting the fish that had been stranded on land by the tidal wave. The muskrats were back mending their lodges; the red-winged blackbirds were calling and wheeling up and over the channels. The geese were *honk-a-lonk*ing. Life in the tidal marshes has adapted over the millennia to the ravages of sea and storm and wind. Everything was back to normal.

A zestful odor reached the nose of the spike buck. He turned his head. The eight-point buck was coming toward him, his rack spanning thirty-three inches. Once more the young buck ran to the dunes, his white tail flag flying and twitching.

Another year would pass before he would challenge the monarch again. By then he would have shed his spikes in February, and started growing new ones in April. These would branch into antlers with one or two points. As each year passed, they would grow until he carried a great rack like the monarch's. Then he would fight the old buck and win. His fawns would romp in the grasses of Mamacoke Marsh, and his own spike bucks would run from his challenges in September.

The buck walked far down the dunes, then turned inland to another patch of groundsel trees. Here he would wait until the rut was over, and he and the monarch could live in peace. Then he and his herd would trek to the valley in the pines to yard during the ice and snow storms of winter.

The spike buck had met the challenge of the September moon. He probably would live to see sixteen more, for the first year and a half of a deer's life are the hardest. He chewed his cud and watched the moon rise as the sun went down.

THE MOON OF THE ALLIGATORS

Two eyes poked above the still water. Each iris was silver-yellow and each pupil black and narrow. They were the eyes of the alligator of Sawgrass Hole, who was floating like a log on the surface of the water as she watched for food. She saw the blue sky above her, and because her eyes were on the top and to the rear of her head, she saw all the way behind her to the tall cypress trees. Their limbs spread like silver wires above a tangle of sweet bay and buttonbushes.

The alligator did not move, but watched and waited even though hunger gnawed her belly. She had eaten little since June, when the rainy season had flooded her home and the prey she fed upon had swum away. Now her sense of seasonal rhythm told her that the afternoon's cloudless sky meant the end of the rains and hurricanes, and the return of the wildlife to her water hole. The moon of October was the beginning of southern Florida's dry season. The water level would fall. The fish, frogs, turtles, and birds would come back to Sawgrass Hole, where she lived. They would be followed by the herons and ibis, egrets, anhinga or water turkeys, and she would eat well once more.

She was in her pool in the Everglades of Florida, which is not a swamp as it is often called, but a river like none other in the world. The Everglades does not flow—it seeps. Forty to sixty miles wide and a hundred miles long, it creeps, like glistening quicksilver, from Lake Okeechobee southward across a flat limestone bed to the Florida Bay. The Everglades is not only a river, but also a wet prairie. Saw grass, that rugged plant whose glasslike leaves are edged with sharp spines, grows like a crop from shore to shore. Rising out of the saw grass are tree islands, known as hammocks, where a variety of trees grow. Other islands are forests of bay, called "heads," buttonwood and cypress trees.

The Everglades and its plants and creatures, including the alligator, have adapted to the wet and dry seasons of the semitropical zone in south Florida. When the river is high in summer's wet season, little fish, like guppies and gambusia that eat mosquito larvae, swim among the saw grass stalks far out in the river. They dodge the largemouth bass and sunfish, who, in turn, avoid the Florida soft-shelled turtle.

During the winter season when the river is low, the wildlife of the Everglades adjusts to dryness. As the water level drops, and just before the river bottom becomes exposed to the sun and cracks, the river creatures come to the alligator holes. They live through the drought of winter in these watery sanctuaries.

October was always a critical time for the alligators as they waited for their food to return. In this century, however, the month of October has become a near disaster for them. Human-made canals, dug into the limestone to drain the Everglades for farming, have killed off millions and billions of frogs, fish, birds, mammals, and turtles. Their food depleted, the alligators died in huge numbers from starvation. In addition, hunters killed tens of thousands for their valuable skins. The passing of the alligators threatened all the wildlife in the Everglades, for their holes are oases for life during the dry season. The great flocks of beautiful birds were reduced to a few. Fish and turtles died out for lack of winter retreats. The alligator, people began to realize, was the "farmer" that kept the chain of life going.

In the 1970s there were so few American alligators left on this earth that Congress declared it an endangered species, one that is doomed to extinction and would be protected by law. Since that decree, the big reptiles have made a strong comeback in their original homeland that stretches from Texas to North Carolina. They are now only a threatened species.

The six-foot alligator of Sawgrass Hole did not know about her status, she only knew her belly ached. Sinking to the bottom of the pool, she looked for food. The river was getting low. A few minnows too small to bother with darted past her. A measly pollywog rested in the warm mud. She ignored it, whipped her tail from side to side, and then circled her large home. The water was filling

with algae, one-celled plants that grow pro-
fusely in the sun. Long strips of these green
plants floated in scummy masses. They both-
ered her.

With a powerful thrust from her tail she
drove her body into a patch of algae and
caught it on her nose. Swimming with sur-
prising grace, she carried it to the shore and
pushed it up with her nose and feet, then
returned and bulldozed another load ashore.
Next she went to the overgrown water lilies
floating on the surface. Taking a plant in her
mouth, she tugged it across the pool and
dragged it up on land to die.

When she was done she could see the
minnows more clearly, and the minnows,
freed from the weeds, flickered back and forth
across Sawgrass Hole eating microscopic
food called periphyton. In the days that followed, they grew rapidly and larger fish fed on
them. For the alligator, however, there was no

food big enough for her to bother with.

Her hole, which was fifteen feet deep and some forty feet long and wide, was far out in the Everglades at the edge of a cypress head. On one of its shores was a beach where she sunbathed. Around the edges of the pool in the shallow water grew pickerelweed and arrowheads. Among their stems the fry of the largemouth bass grew up. On the shore, just out of the water, grew clumps of six-foot-tall alligator flags. Their large leaves, on the ends of long stalks, waved and fluttered like banners. These plants announce the locations of alligator homes to human, bird, and beast. When the big reptiles are killed or die, the plants die too, for there is no alligator-farmer to weed. The algae multiply and clog the pools, weeds take over the shallows and shore and, finally, trees and bushes fill in the pond, choking out the alligator flags.

One evening the big 'gator lay near the

shore watching the bushes. The moon of October was working its change. The water in the river was lowering, and the fish and wildlife were coming to her deep hole. A snowy egret alighted on a limb of a pop ash near the water. The bird no longer held his feathers close to his body as he did in summer, but lifted them slightly to let his delicate plumes float down the back of his neck like a veil. The moon of October is the beginning of the breeding season for the egrets. In a month or so he would strut for his mate, spread his plumes, then bow and dance for her.

The egret picked up a stick, held it a moment, then dropped it. It was a present for his mate, but he was not quite ready to give it to her. October was a time to practice the art of courtship, and practice he did. He picked up another stick. The alligator eyed him but did not stalk. He was too high in the tree to catch.

The bird flew, his yellow feet and black legs gleaming as he skimmed over Sawgrass Hole and climbed into the air. High over the 'gator hole, he turned and headed for his rookery on a buttonwood island near the Florida Bay. The 'gator watched him until he was out of sight, then submerged herself in the river. She made no ripples to alarm her prey, nor did she disturb the waters as she pressed her huge jaws together. They closed over seventy sharp white teeth, forming the perpetual grin of an alligator. Her tail, almost half of her length, torpedoed her across the pool to the shore where the cypress trees grew. As she came up on land, water spilled from her sculptured armor and her third eyelid pulled back to let her see in the air.

The alligator saw movement beneath a pop ash. Rising to her feet on short legs, she peered into a brushy jungle that she and her ancestors had created. For a thousand years the alligators of Sawgrass Hole had made land by weeding and piling the debris on this shore. Tree seeds had rooted in the rich compost. The seedlings had grown into a sheltering jungle that attracted rabbits, raccoons, bobcats, and river otter.

The 'gator lunged at a marsh rabbit who was nibbling on leaves. He had been born in late summer. With the rise of the moon of October he had left home to seek his fortune. He had not gone far before he came upon the alligator's jungle and, finding it rich with rabbit food, settled in. Blackish-brown in color, he looked like the cottontail rabbits of the north, except that he had no white on his tail. However, he did possess their ability to leap, and before the alligator could lunge a second time, he had catapulted over her tail and plunged into the pool. He swam quickly across Sawgrass Hole and bounced ashore. Marsh rabbits are excellent swimmers.

Being so close to catching a rabbit made the alligator even hungrier. She dove into her pool and scanned the undersides of the bladderworts, floating plants that catch insects and take nourishment from them. No dark areas marked the bodies of resting frogs. They were still out in the glades. Patiently she waited.

Days passed. Her hunger increased.

One morning she crawled onto her sunny beach to warm her muscles. The nights were cooler now, and since alligators are cold-blooded animals, she depended on the sun to warm her up. After basking for an hour she started off into the saw grass to look for food. The trail she took was as old as her pool. A raised roadbed, it consisted of dead saw grass, trampled by generations of alligators traveling from Sawgrass Hole to the glades and islands. The path was used heavily. In April the bull alligators from tens of miles around came down it to breed the females of Sawgrass Hole. In summer and fall when food was scarce the females and young walked the path to hammocks and moats.

The alligator moved more slowly on land than in water, yet she covered the mile to the edge of her territory long before noon. Hunger was driving her swiftly to the hardwood hammock to hunt.

Hammocks are not like any other islands. They are greenhouses on rock outcrops in the "river of grass," and they are mysteriously beautiful. Handsome hardwood trees, live oaks, gumbo-limbos, mastics, and mahoganies grow there. Orchids, air plants, ferns, and mosses festoon the tree limbs and trunks. Since no drying winds penetrate the dense canopy of the hammocks, the air inside is moist and warm, as in a greenhouse, and the plants grow in profusion.

The alligator climbed ashore. She pushed

between red maples and pop ashes at the edge of the hammock and entered a large, dimly lit forest. A bobcat was sleeping on the broad limb of a live oak. He did not run when he saw the alligator, nor did she when she saw the cat. Bobcats and big alligators have no enemies but humans.

She rounded a mossy log and came to a stop. Her reptilian memory recognized a limb of the live oak above her and warned her of an old disaster. She lay still.

The fear passed and she walked on. Within a few feet she saw the greenish-yellow flowers of the butterfly orchid. A warning bell rang in her brain and again she stopped. Cautiously she looked around. A snow-white ghost orchid bloomed at her side. She recalled having seen that before too. The grass ferns that hung from a sable palm like a beard were also familiar. On a log the resurrection ferns, now curling up to live out the dry season, warned her to go back. Once she had met trouble here. She stopped her trek.

Hunger overcame her fear and she started off again. A flock of warblers dropped down from the canopy where they had been feeding and flew over the pineapplelike bromeliads on the ground. The little birds were migrating from New England and Canada to Mexico and South America. Every October they stopped in the hammocks of the Everglades to feed on the abundant insects. The presence of the warblers also sent a message of warning to the alligator, but she was painfully hungry.

She walked toward a deep hole she remembered. It was one of the many holes in the Everglades leached out of the limestone by the acids from decaying plants. They are called solution holes. This one was twenty feet across, fifteen feet deep, round and straight-sided like a well. It was filled with water to its fern-trimmed top. In its depths swam huge garfish. When they were very small, they had entered the solution hole through Swiss cheese-like openings that pock the limestone. Then they had grown too big to swim out. The alligator saw them, but hesitated to dive into the hole. A fuzzy memory held her back.

The sun went down suddenly as it does in the semitropics and the big reptile lay still. Her upper and lower lids closed over her bright eyes and she slept.

The moon came up. The raccoons walked up and down tree limbs catching tree frogs. Some romped along the water edge hunting for crayfish. The bobcat awoke and continued his solitary trek across the October glades. He had left his mother and his brother a year ago, and would live alone until late December, when he would find a female of his choice and mate. He would not stay with her long, for like most cats, he was a solitary animal.

At dawn the alligator looked into the solution hole again, and again she did not dive in. Her reptilian mind was clicking off memories of another October when she had been younger.

Her life had begun in August buried under a pile of warm, decaying vegetation near Sawgrass Hole. The mound, a nest, was eight to ten feet wide and five feet high. Even while she was still inside her egg, the baby alligator heard her mother grunting and calling to her. With great effort, she struggled out of her brittle eggshell and clawed her way up through the debris toward the sound. As she neared the surface, her mother's scaly foot gently pulled back the vegetation, and the baby alligator scrambled into August's steamy heat. She was eight inches long.

She was joined by thirty-nine other baby alligators, who, like herself, looked exactly like their parents, except for their round knobby heads and the bright-yellow spots on the end of each body scale. Full of spirit, the babies began to snap at each other as they ran to their grunting mother. When all were free of the nest, she led them toward the water as fast as she was able. Baby alligators have many enemies.

Even on that first day of life the hatchling alligator was a survivor. Sensing danger, she marched under the protection of her mother's jaw. This was wise. No sooner had she and her tribe reached the trail to Sawgrass Hole than a great blue heron dropped out of the sky. He ate two babies before their mother could grab him in her teeth. Then swiftly, as if word of the hatchlings had been broadcast across the Everglades, the herons and hawks arrived to prey on them. A black snake slipped down a live oak tree, snatched one and swallowed it. A raccoon, hearing the mother alligator grunting and the birds screaming, came down from the same tree and grabbed a straggler.

When the baby alligator reached Sawgrass Hole there were only twenty-three of the forty alive. Since she was one of them, she continued to stay close to her mother. She entered the water under her jaw and stayed there while the lively flotilla of big and little 'gators crossed the pond. Bright flecks of sunlight danced on the surface of the water and strange water beetles scooted past her.

Tiny fish darted by. Instinctively the baby snapped at them, but did not come out from under her mother. She stayed right where she was until they reached a cave. It had been chewed, clawed, and scraped into existence by the female alligators of Sawgrass Hole to protect their babies from predators. The little alligator scrambled out of the water and lay down on a narrow beach far back in the cave. She was very tired.

For the next nine months the baby 'gator swam in and out of the cave catching minnows and bugs. She ate well and avoided her enemies. By April she was eighteen inches long and too big for the predators to attack her.

Nevertheless she stayed with her mother until another year passed. One day a huge bull 'gator came to Sawgrass Hole. He swam, rolled, and splashed with her mother. He bellowed mating cries that could be heard a mile away. After a few weeks he departed and the alligator's mother was no longer friendly to her. She attacked her now three-foot-long daughter frequently. One night she drove her out of Sawgrass Hole. The mother's loyalty lay with a new clutch of eggs in a new nest.

The young alligator followed the family trail through the saw grass and moved into a moat at the edge of the very hammock she was on now. She felt the river rise and watched the fish and turtles swim away. Food became scarce. Then October came and the river began to drop. One afternoon the alligator went into the hammock to hunt. She walked beneath the orchids and the mahogany trees, she saw the warblers, passed the butterfly orchid and discovered the solution hole. It was filled with trapped fish. Without hesitating, she splashed into its waters and before sunset was full and content.

For a month she lived well on the garfish. Then, out of food, restless to move on, she tried to climb out. She could not. The water had dropped too low; the steep sides of the solution hole were impossible to climb.

The alligator was trapped. She saw the warblers leave, she saw the air plants bloom on the live oak limb overhead, and she saw the world above her grow smaller and smaller as the water dropped her deeper and deeper into the dark pit. Finally, only the tip of the oak limb was visible above her, and she was on the dry bottom of the solution hole without food or water.

By spring she was starving to death. Then one night a marsh rabbit, who was running away from a bobcat, fell into the hole. Several weeks later an armadillo tumbled down to her. Deep in the solution hole, the young alligator existed on chance while stoically waiting for life or death.

June brought the rains back. Clouds gathered, lightning flashed, and torrents fell from dark thunderheads. The solution hole began to fill with water. One day a veritable deluge of rain poured into the hole and lifted her to the top. Mustering what little energy she had left, she crawled out of her prison and dragged herself home to Sawgrass Hole.

When she had reached her home, she paused. Something was wrong. Algae and weeds filled her pool. The alligator flags were dead.

The once-clear water was green. Snapping turtles haunted the murky depths, for there were no alligators in Sawgrass Hole to keep them in check. Human poachers had found the ancestral home and killed all the magnificent reptiles.

The young alligator went to work. Eagerly she ate the turtles and weeded the pond. The fish returned, the birds came to eat the fish, and the mammals arrived to catch the birds. When Sawgrass Hole was clear of weeds, the alligator flags again brightened its edges with their flashy leaves.

That had been three years ago. Now on the edge of that same solution hole, the alligator was remembering, in her reptilian way, that she should not go after the fish. Torn between her terrible hunger and her sense of survival, she simply lay still. That evening a family of raccoons approached the hole. She lunged at them. Three jumped into the solution hole, swam and climbed safely out. A fourth ran down the trail, with the alligator lumbering after it. Although she could move as swiftly as a closing switchblade when she was close to an animal, she was no match for a running raccoon.

And now, since she faced homeward, she kept on going. She pushed between the red maples, swam across the moat, and took the ancestral trail to Sawgrass Hole.

She slid into the water. Even in her short absence things had changed. The water had dropped three inches. Large patches of algae had died and taken oxygen from the water as they decayed. Hundreds of minnows had suffocated.

Once more the alligator went to work— dragging, pushing, and bulldozing weeds to let the sunlight into her pool. This year there were no big turtles to eat and her hunger increased.

When the moon arose at the end of October, her home was ready to receive the migrants from the drying river. Her pool sparkled. Presently little bass and garfish wiggled into the clear water through holes in the limestone. Snails became abundant at the edge of Sawgrass Hole as they sought the stems of the moist plants that grew there.

Three egrets came to the pond to fish in the shallows. The following afternoon five arrived, then twenty-five. Behind them many big turtles were plodding slowly toward the fresh water. Purple gallinules arrived to eat the water beetles, and the bobcat came in to eat the gallinules. Little fish ate the microscopic creatures of the pond, big fish ate little fish, and the alligator would eat the big fish.

When the moon of October was waning, the leaves of the cypress began to fall. The foliage of the persimmon and maple trees, migrants from the north, turned gold and

Canada geese head for shore.

An adult buck must scare off his challenger.

Sal Catalano

The young buck has grown his first antlers.

The alligator watches and waits, looking for food.

The alligator is trapped.

Sal Catalano

All year the caribou travel,
wandering almost four hundred miles.

The wolves' voices carry across the mountains.

The wolf pack tracks a caribou.

Sal Catalano

red. They would remain leafless for a few weeks in deference to their heredity, then bud, leaf, and flower again. The autumn that is so brilliant in the north is hardly noticeable in the semitropics. It is only a pause in the cycle.

Life was returning but the alligator still had no food. Although the bass were growing rapidly, they were not large enough to eat, and the wood storks, who were big, managed to stay clear of her jaws.

She watched the small frogs swim and catch insects. Cricket frogs, tree frogs, little glass frogs, pig frogs, and leopard frogs were food for the raccoons and birds, but not for her.

A crayfish that had lived all summer under the moist root of the cypress stalked to the pond bank and began picking up clumps of marl in its claws. These it placed in a pile. Digging and scooping, it cut itself a tunnel to the water and, backing down the tunnel, entered Sawgrass Hole, where it would feast on snails and dead fish. Other crayfish joined it.

At the end of October the river dropped still farther. The canal locks were opened to drain the land for the human farmers.

One morning the hungry reptile left her cave swimming slowly, for she was cold from the night air. She was headed for her beach to warm up in the sun. Suddenly she whipped her tail and lunged. A huge turtle had arrived in the pool. She slammed her jaws shut. Her long fast was over. More turtles and big garfish were swimming into her hole from the drying glades.

When the moon of November rose, the alligator of Sawgrass Hole lay on her beach, a fixed smile on her face.

THE MOON OF THE GRAY WOLVES

S now shot through Toklat Pass on a wail-
ing wind that twisted trees and tore at
rocks. The wind ripped the snowfall from the
alpine slopes and plastered it against the steep
face of Mount Sheldon in the Alaska Range.
These gargantuan mountains of rock and ice
spear the sky north of Anchorage and south
of the mighty Yukon River. Their peaks and
valleys shelter the royalty of North American
mammals: the grizzly bear, Dall sheep,
moose, elk, caribou, and the magnificent wolf.

In Toklat Pass the moon of November
rose in darkness although it was only four

o'clock in the afternoon. The sun sets early and rises late. Mount Sheldon would not see the sun until a few hours before noon the next day.

In the faint light of a crescent moon a large black wolf lifted his nose from his warm tail and sniffed the subzero air. He was the leader of the wolf pack of Toklat River, the leader of four other adults and five pups. Snow crystals clung to his magnificent ruff as he got lightly to his feet. He shook himself and trotted into the blasting wind. Head up, eyes squinted, he fought his way to the knoll above his sleeping pack. They were covered with snow and curled like furry knots on this promontory above the Toklat River. Wagging his tail in pleasure, the black wolf studied his team. He could see them well in the dark. Yellow rods in his eyes absorbed the light from the night's clouds, stars, and moon, and reflected it back onto his retina, making sight possible in the night. The scents and gentle breathing of his mate, his pups, and his three adult helpers aided him in seeing his pack quite clearly.

The moon of November would test the pups for their ability to survive. Few would pass. Only the healthiest and most intelligent would live through the first year. The adults could not coddle them now.

From May to November the adult wolves of the Toklat River pack had cared for the pups. Now they were full-grown and must take their chances against slashing caribou and moose hooves, crevasses and avalanches, disease and accidents. They would be shot at by human beings, who competed with them for game and sold their radiant furs. The life of a wolf is hard and dangerous.

Only a hundred years ago gray wolves roamed across Canada, Alaska, and most of the contiguous United States where wildlife flourished. Ill adapted to civilization, they departed for wilder places. Today the only wolves in the lower forty-eight states hide out in the deep wilderness of Michigan and Minnesota. Canada has a healthy number of wolves, as does Alaska, but Alaska sets no limits for hunting them, and in some areas their numbers are declining.

Standing on the knoll in the wind, the black wolf pricked his ears forward. The frozen valley floor crackled with the activity of caribou, the North American cousin of the Eurasian reindeer. A herd of bulls, with their picturesque branching antlers, had come through Toklat Pass during the day. They were bedding down on the flats near the river. Two thousand strong, they had recently left the slopes of Mount McKinley, the tallest of North American mountains, where their food—the grasses, willow, and dwarf birch leaves—was dying in winter's darkness and cold. Beneath the moon that would test the wolf pups, the caribou were on their way to the lichens in the valley of the Yukon River two hundred miles away. The cows and calves would soon be following the bulls to new foods. The moon of November would also be a test for the caribou.

Caribou are wanderers. All year they circle from one food source to the next, eating, mating, and giving birth as they tread their unending route. This herd was a small fraction of the twenty to thirty thousand caribou in Denali National Park. With the coming of November, after circling a range three to four hundred miles in diameter—which would be the distance from New York City to Pittsburgh, Pennsylvania, or from Quebec City to Gaspé in the Province of Quebec—they were back at Toklat River, where they started.

The black wolf threw back his head and

howled a melodious song. His mate, the silver wolf and the leader of the females and pups, answered him. When she was done, the vice-president of the pack sang his aria. He was followed by the young female, who had left her family to join the Toklat River pack. Finally, the old wolf sang out. Then all howled in harmony. If one wolf joined another's note, the first would shift to a new note. Each wanted to express himself with his own individual music, particularly in this, the call-to-action song. It was like a cheer at a football pep rally, "go, win, go." The wolves of Toklat River sang with great exuberance and anticipation this night. They were out on the promontory living the gypsy life of the wolves again.

The five adult wolves had been confined to a small area since the pups were born in May. Except for hunting the river valley, they had remained close to the old family den. It went twelve feet into the hillside and was used year after year by the wolves of Toklat River. Wildflowers brightened its entrance. For two weeks the mother had remained in the den with the pups, for they were born helpless and blind and needed constant care. During this time the black wolf brought his mate food, placing it far down the tunnel where she could reach it without disturbing the pups. Sometimes the father would wait in the tunnel until he heard them whimper. Then he would back out wagging his tail furiously. The other members of the pack would see his "smiling" tail that said the pups were fine and well and they, too, would wag their tails.

One twilight when the sun had been shining almost all day, the pups stepped cautiously out of the den. The adults pranced and howled at the sight of them. They sniffed their little noses in greeting and wagged their tails joyously. Wolves love their pups.

During the long hours of daylight in June the pups pounced on bobbing flowers, chased Arctic ground squirrels, and played games like king-of-the-hill and tug-of-war with bones. When their mother went hunting, one of the other adults would baby-sit. Wolves never leave their pups unattended.

In early August, when the pups could tear meat, the black wolf led his pack to their summer home. This was another den used year after year, but a simpler one. It was a tunnel in the middle of a vast alpine meadow. Here the pups could hide when they were tired or frightened, and here, high above the valley, the adults could watch for food: caribou, moose, deer, and Dall sheep. Wolves prey on big game. They take the sick, and the old, and young and, by harvesting these, keep the wild animals in balance with their food supply. When big game is scarce, the wolf will take marmots, ground squirrels, and even rabbits and lemmings. In the scheme of things, however, these little animals are the natural food of the coyote and fox, the smaller members of the Canidae, or dog family.

One September night the black wolf sat down by the summer den, lifted his head, and howled a song of change. It sounded across the peaks and valleys like a plaintive woodwind instrument. When the song ended, the black leader dashed out over the alpine tundra and up the ridges of the mountain. Life at the summer den was over.

That night the air bit cold, the leaves were long gone from the willows, and the grizzly bears and marmots were in their dens. The black wolf ran at the head of his pack, dashing through snow patches, climbing ridges, and chasing across the flats of his vast territory that reached from Mount Sheldon to and beyond the park boundary—caribou land. At sunup they ran out on a rocky promontory and stopped. Wagging their tails, they scratched out saucer-shaped beds under the cold stars and lay down to sleep. The nomadic life of the wolves had begun.

This night in November they were back on that same promontory, a favorite site of the black wolf's because he could survey the river valley from here. He tensed his muscles. A lone caribou, who had gotten separated from the herd, was coming through Toklat Pass.

The black wolf planned a strategy to take the prey.

He was a thousand feet above timberline, the line where the trees stop growing and the tundra takes over. In the Alaska Range the timberline begins a mere 2,500 to 3,000 feet above sea level. The farther north from the Alaska Range, the lower the timberline becomes. In the Arctic Circle, some two hundred miles above the Alaska Range, there are no trees at all. The ground is permanently frozen and only grasses and short-rooted herbs survive.

In the black wolf's territory the trees grew along the rivers and streams. The ice and wind had stunted the trees and clipped them short, and so the black wolf could see right over them into Toklat Pass. The caribou was a female. Her antlers were small compared to those of a bull. She walked in comfort in the fierce cold, for the hair of the caribou is partly hollow, forming a dead air space, which is the best insulation known to man or beast.

A pup yipped, the wrong thing to do when a leader is watching prey. The caribou heard and bolted back down the pass.

The black wolf was not perturbed. There would be others. He returned to his pack and was greeted by his mate. He took her muzzle gently in his mouth to say he was the leader of the pack. She licked his cheek and chin to say he was, indeed, the leader. The other adults paid homage to him in the same manner, and as they did so, the needs of the pack inspired him: food, companionship, and teamwork. He lifted his head and tail above them in the pose of the loving leader. Wolves have many ways of communicating with each other. Posturing, voice, eye contact, and scent are their languages. With these tools they say all that is necessary for wolf life.

The pups ran to their father. His ears twitched fondly. His tail wagged furiously. Their ears and tails went down to say that he was their leader.

For a moment he studied them. They were still floppy and loose. Pack work would be hard on them, especially on the mindless one who had yipped and scared the caribou, and the lanky one who often tripped over his own feet. Only last night, as he had tracked a porcupine out on the frozen river, he had stumbled and slid, nearly falling into a hole made by a moose who had just broken through the thin ice at the river's bend.

The pups bounced and yipped. The leader was enjoying their enthusiasm, but the old wolf was annoyed. To escape them he trotted to the knoll and scanned Toklat Pass through his sharply slanted eyes. A year ago in September he had joined the pack. His mate had been shot and his pups had joined other packs. For two months he had lived alone near the top of Mount Sheldon. There, a wolf without a pack could capture the lambs of the Dall sheep and the slow-moving marmots. One night he heard the wolves of Toklat River playing by their summer den. He yearned for company. At dawn he trotted up to the black wolf, head low, tail between his legs. This pose said to the leader that he would be submissive and work well as long as the black wolf would have him. With a wag of the tail, the leader took him in.

As the old wolf watched the pass, the young female paid homage to the leader. Too young to have pups herself last May, she had hidden in the wide corridor between her parents' pack and the pack of Toklat River. No wolves trespass in this area except to hide and wait to be invited into a pack. The corridor prevents wolf fights and inadvertently protects the game. One night the silver wolf saw the young female in the corridor and called her out to hunt with her. She ran a tasty hare to the silver wolf. At the end of the night the silver wolf led the young female to the Toklat River den. The silver wolf made all the decisions where females and pups were concerned, and some of the hunting decisions, too. At her command the young female stayed home with the pups when she went hunting with the pack. During the long hours that she was baby-sitting, the young female taught the pups to pounce by swishing her tail for them to jump on. She let them practice their hunting skills by wrestling with them and letting them chase and pounce on her. Taking care of wolf pups is a strenuous job.

The gray wolf was the leader's brother. They had grown up together on the Toklat wolf range. There was no question of who was the dominant one of the two when they were pups. The black wolf was a born leader. Larger than his brother, he was completely fearless. When a strange animal approached, he ran right up to it. He initiated all the games and chases, and he was persistent. He would stick with a job longer than his littermates, whether it was digging a hole or chasing butterflies. He had all the qualities of leadership—fearlessness, initiative, and diligence. He was an intelligent, strong leader, but he depended on his vice-president brother to work with him for success.

The black wolf joined the old wolf on the

promontory edge. He sat down and threw back his head as he howled the opening call of the hunt song. His vice-president brother joined him in song, then the pack sang, and the pups yipped. Their voices carried out across the mountains and down through the pass.

The black-and-white magpies sleeping in the spruce trees along the river opened their eyes. They would listen to the wolves this night. The hunt song meant food for them. The ravens in the crags of Toklat Pass heard the song. They lifted their feathers in contentment. Wolf leftovers were also raven delights.

The rock ptarmigans below the promontory wiggled deeper into the snow and then did not move. The last of their summer plumage had molted, and they were as white as the world they lived in and almost impossible to see. The snowshoe hares who heard the song pressed their ears closer to their heads and burrowed into the snowdrifts. Porcupines climbed higher in the trees along the river, and a pair of foxes sneaked out on a ledge and watched the wolves. Like the ravens and magpies, the foxes enjoyed the scraps of a wolf feast, too.

The black wolf ended the song and plunged off the ledge. The moon of November was upon the land. His pack followed him down the wind-cleared slope where it seemed no life could survive. Yet they passed creatures who live all winter in the snow and cold. Lemmings ran their tunnels, ground squirrels and marmots hibernated beneath the soil, and two snowy owls sat on top of the snow. The black wolf glanced at the owls as he ran, holding his head high in the manner of the leader. They had come down from the treeless tundra near Point Barrow, where they had hatched in June in a nest on the ground.

In the constant daylight of the Arctic

summer the parents of these owls had hunted the abundant lemmings. Millions of the little furry rodents ran through the grass, eating, building nests, breeding, giving birth to thirteen young at a time, who in a few weeks gave birth to thirteen more, who gave birth to thirteen more until there were too many lemmings. They crowded each other, and in doing so they released a chemical into their bloodstream that made them so restless they ran this way and that. The foxes, owls, gulls, weasels, wolves—every creature that eats meat—fed on them until almost all were gone. A few survived to start the cycle again. The young owls, their food depleted by the normal cycles in nature, took off early for their wintering grounds in the Alaska Range. Some of their relatives would go on into Canada and a rare few as far south as Texas. The two passing over Toklat Pass saw the wolves running and flew down onto the snow. They were not above eating wolf leftovers either.

Breaking into a graceful gallop, the black wolf led his pack across the valley. As they leaped a log, the lanky pup stumbled. The black wolf looked back at him, lifted his lips, and snarled in contempt. The pup whimpered and fell in behind the vice-president to copy an expert stride and learn.

Near the river they swerved to avoid the tight tangles of cranberries, rhododendrons, and crowberries, then entered the stubby spruce forest that edged the Toklat River. They ran swiftly although it was dark under the trees and the snow very deep. The pups struggled; the old wolf panted. The black wolf slowed down to accommodate them.

Fur swinging under their bellies, ruffs blowing in the wind, the pack fought their way to the willow and alder trees that grow at the water's edge. Weaving between these, they slipped out onto the ice and sped off, galloping again. The old wolf had caught his second wind and the pups were free of the deep snow. The night was electric with caribou scent. They ran in silence looking from right to left for a straggler. So perfectly were they moving, one behind another, that when they passed, it looked as if but one wolf had been on the river. All nine had stepped in their leader's tracks.

Their pace was a moderate fifteen miles an hour when the lanky pup stumbled again. The black wolf looked back at him. Diverted, he did not pick up the faint odor of a moose and her calf bedded down in the alders on the shore. She, however, knew the wolves were running and was about to rise and bolt when the black wolf turned his head, missed her scent, and ran on. When the wolves were far down the river, the moose blew air out of her nostrils to tell her big calf all was well. He snorted an answer from the edge of the grove.

On the frozen river the black wolf picked up the odor of a caribou ahead. This was what he was looking for, a lone animal. The herd was too dangerous to tackle. He glanced at his vice-president and signaled him by eye contact to move out to the left. With another glance he sent his mate to the right. Then he charged. The two outposts charged. The young female and the old wolf followed. The pups ran behind.

The wolves were down to business, and the wild things knew it. The massive wolverine, walking his lonely trail, pulled into a hollow until they passed. The willow ptarmigans that were flocking by the thousands along the river shifted in the dark. Above them sat a gyrfalcon waiting for the sun. All were aware that the wolves were hunting. A great number of lives were tied closely to the lives of the wolves.

The caribou scent led the black wolf off

the river ice into the forest. By now he knew much about his quarry, for scent is perhaps the most vivid language of the wolves. The animal was a bull, and odorously old. Like other male caribou at this time of year, he smelled lean. During the breeding season—from mid-September to the end of October—bulls do not eat, and end the period thin and gaunt. This animal was not well. His urine told of functional weakness.

The black wolf signaled his pack to "exert," then led them through deep drifts. They sank to their chests and lost ground. The caribou made headway. He was designed to travel in these conditions. His huge hooves were like snowshoes that held him up on the crust. Sick though he was, he soon left the wolves far behind.

The wolf pack came to the top of a ridge. The male caribou was ahead of them, too far away to catch. The black wolf did not go on.

The old wolf and the pups were tired, and—one pup was missing. The mindless one had fallen into a hole in the river. The black wolf and his mate did not go back to look for her. The moon of November was selecting the pups.

The adults made beds on the hilltop. The pups simply fell in the snow and put their noses in their tails. The lanky pup dropped beside his father. The chase had been long and strenuous. The black wolf glanced at him. The stumbler might be the next victim of the moon of November.

A few hours before sunup a whistling wind awoke the black wolf. He stretched and slowly got to his feet.

The river valley was bright with red, yellow, green, blue, and violet lights. He looked up. A fountain of color shot up in the sky and fell back. The aurora borealis was crackling over the Yukon River. Charged particles given off by the sun in a solar flare had been trapped some one hundred miles above the North Pole by the Van Allen belt of radiation. Drawn into curtainlike patterns by the Earth's magnetic field, the particles collide with air molecules and become luminous. The black wolf used the light of the aurora to scan the valley. His eyes focused. His ears shot forward. In the willows on the other side of the river a large beast was walking.

He howled urgently. The vice-president and his silver mate sprung to his side; the old wolf joined them. The lanky pup, sensing the excitement, chased his tail, then fell into line behind his mother, the young female, and the other pups. They flowed down the slope. At the river's edge a flock of juncos beat their wings frantically in the darkness. The birds had nested by the mountain streams in the summer, flocked by the thousands in September, and were now overnighting as they made their way south to prairies, gardens, and fields in Canada and the lower forty-eight states.

The pack paid no attention to the juncos, but a red fox did. A frightened bird lost its footing in the dark and fluttered down to him.

The wolf pack crossed the river at twenty-two miles an hour. Like one streaming beast it shot up the bank and sped into the willows where the caribou was walking. It was a young bull that was weakened by parasites. The black wolf circled. The caribou thundered out into the open, where he could run faster than the wolves.

The black wolf did not try to catch up with the speeding bull; rather, he set a steady pace that his pack could keep up all night and the next day, if necessary. The caribou, he knew from experience, could not run fast for long. He would dash swiftly, then rest. With each rest, the wolves, who were steadily, relentlessly trotting along, would gain on the prey.

When, at last, the bull was too tired to sprint, the wolves closed in on him.

The black wolf glanced at his mate. She dashed ahead and stood in front of the tired caribou, who turned to run the other way only to face the black wolf. Another command from his leader—and the old wolf charged. He snapped at the caribou's legs. The bull reared and slashed at him with his razor-sharp hooves, narrowly missing a pup. The black wolf rushed for the animal's vulnerable side and signaled his vice-president to close in with him.

Suddenly the lanky pup bolted forward to help his father. He stumbled. The caribou lowered his piercing antlers and charged the pup. Instantly the black wolf leaped between the pup and the bull and was hooked on the shoulder. With a swing of his powerful neck the buck tossed the wolf through the air. Falling onto the snow, the wolf rolled head over heels, then flipped to his feet. Stunned, he stood still for several minutes. As he got his bearings, he heard the snarl of the kill.

Now there was food for all. The black wolf trotted to the feast.

Some hours later the pack was comfortably full, yet good meat remained. Picking up a portion, the silver wolf carried it to the edge of the forest, dug a hole, and buried it. The young female cached other pieces, and the pups stuffed bits under logs and bushes. Much of the kill still lay on the snow when the pack went off to the promontory to sleep for the day. The white gyrfalcon awoke and sped down Toklat Pass looking for birds.

When the moon set, shortly after sunup, the black wolf licked his bruised shoulder and surveyed his pack. All were asleep but the lanky pup, who was staring devotedly at him. The black wolf wagged his tail and sighed. His pack was splendid. Even the lanky pup was daring, if not perfect. He might live through the winter after all.

The wind blew in strong gusts as the sun—cold, gold, and heatless—came over the mountains and shone down on the sleeping wolves, who were almost entirely covered with wind-blown snow.

The magpies awoke. They shook out their feathers and yawned. One hopped up through the limbs to the top of a spruce. He looked for the signs of the wolf kill he had heard in the night. Unable to locate it, he took to his wings. Flying high, he saw the torn snow, the fur, and the tasty leftovers. He circled down to the kill. Three more magpies joined him; then from twigs and limbs dozens flew down to eat.

Winging to the feast came two ravens. They had seen the magpies and then the kill from a rocky perch on Mount Sheldon. When the ravens arrived, the magpies flew off and sat some distance from them on the snow. The ravens were the dominant birds at the feast. As at a state dinner, the birds and beasts seat themselves by rank.

A bald eagle soaring high above the pass saw the ravens and magpies on the snow and flew down to the kill. The ravens stepped aside for him, but not very far. A fox family came to the feast.

The wolves of Toklat River had provided a banquet for the inhabitants of Toklat Valley.

As the sun reached its low apogee and started down the sky, the black wolf glanced down at the party. He was not possessive about his food. He did not have to be. Other weakened caribou lingered along the river, and the cows and calves would soon be coming through. Above him the hooves of the Dall sheep clanked on the rocks, and moose walked in the willows. Food was abundant for the wolves of Toklat River.

And—four of the five pups had passed the first test of the moon of November.

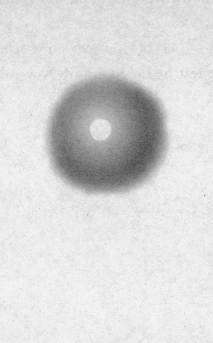

BIBLIOGRAPHY

Adler, C. S. *Carly's Buck.* New York: Clarion Books, 1987.

Ahlstrom, Mark E. *The Whitetail.* Riverside, N.J.: Crestwood House, 1983.

Arnosky, Jim. *Deer at the Brook.* New York: Lothrop, Lee & Shepard Company, 1985.

Bailey, Jill. *Discovering Deer.* New York: The Bookwright Press, 1988.

Barrett, Norma S. *Crocodiles and Alligators.* Mankato, Minn.: Crestwood House, 1984.

Bender, Lionel. *Crocodiles and Alligators.* New York: Gloucester Press, 1988.

Burt, William H., and Richard P. Grossenheider. *A Field Guide to the Mammals.* The Peterson Field Guide Series. Boston: Houghton Mifflin Company, 1976.

Carner, Chas. *Tawny.* New York: The Macmillan Company, 1978.

Carrick, Donald. *Harald and the Great Stag.* New York: Clarion Books, 1988.

Clarkson, Ewan. *Wolves.* Milwaukee, Wis.: Raintree Children's Books, 1980.

Cloudsley-Thompson, J. L. *Crocodiles & Alligators.* Milwaukee, Wis.: Raintree Children's Books, 1980.

Conant, Roger. *A Field Guide to Reptiles and Amphibians of Eastern Central North America,* The Peterson Field Guide Series. Boston: Houghton Mifflin Company, 1975.

Fox, Dr. Michael. *The Wolf.* New York: Coward, McCann & Geoghegan, 1973.

Gamlin, Linda. *The Deer in the Forest.* Milwaukee, Wis.: Stevens Publishers, 1988.

George, Jean Craighead. *Everglades Wildguide.* Natural History Series. Office of Publications, National

Park Service, U.S. Department of the Interior.
Superintendent of Documents, U.S. Printing
Office, Washington, D.C. 20402. Stock No.
2405–00497.

————. *Julie of the Wolves.* New York: Harper & Row,
1972.

————. *The Wounded Wolf.* New York: Harper & Row,
1978.

Graham, Ada and Frank. *Alligators.* New York:
Delacorte Press, 1979.

Hartley, William B. and Ellen. *The Alligator, King of the
Wilderness.* Camden, N.J.: Thomas Nelson & Sons,
1977.

Hogan, Paula Z. *The Wolf.* Milwaukee, Wis.: Raintree
Children's Books, 1979.

Johnson, Sylvia. *Wolf Pack: Tracking Wolves in the Wild.*
Minneapolis, Minn.: Lerner Publications, 1985.

LaBastille, Anne. *Whitetailed Deer.* Vienna, Va.:
National Wildlife Federation, 1977.

Lopez, Barry Holstun. *Of Wolves and Men.* New York: Charles Scribner's Sons, 1978.

McClung, Robert M. *Whitetail.* New York: William Morrow & Company, Inc., 1987.

McConoughey, Jana. *The Wolves.* Mankato, Minn.: Crestwood House, 1983.

Macdonald, David. *The Encyclopedia of Mammals.* New York: Facts on File, Inc., 1966.

Mech, David L. *The Wolf.* New York: The Natural History Press, 1970.

Moon, Cliff. *Alligators and Crocodiles in the Wild.* Hove, England: Wayland, 1984.

Morrison, Susan Dudley. *The Alligator.* Mankato, Minn.: Crestwood House, 1984.

Palmer, Ralph S. *The Mammal Guide.* Garden City, N.Y.: Doubleday & Company, 1954.

Paulsen, Gary. *Tracker.* New York: Bradbury Press, 1984.

Pringle, Laurence P. *Wolfman: Exploring the World of Wolves.* New York: Charles Scribner's Sons, 1983.

Pruitt, Jim, and Nancy McGowan. *The North American Alligator.* Austin, Tex.: Steck-Vaughn Co., 1974.

Rawlings, Marjorie Kinnan. *The Yearling.* New York: Charles Scribner's Sons, 1985.

Salton, Felix. *Bambi: A Life in the Woods.* New York: Pocket Books, 1988.

Scott, Jack Denton. *Alligator.* New York: G. P. Putnam's Sons, 1984.

Shaw, Evelyn. *Alligators.* New York: Harper & Row, 1972.

Zim, Herbert S. *Alligators and Crocodiles.* New York: William Morrow & Company, Inc., 1978.

INDEX